CW01512503

Original title:
Flickering Fae Among the Moon Verge

Author: Paula Raudsepp
ISBN HARDBACK: 978-1-80559-208-2
ISBN PAPERBACK: 978-1-80559-707-0

Guardians of the Nocturnal Dreamscape

In shadows deep, the lanterns glow,
Whispers weave where night winds blow.
Stars above, like gems in seam,
Guardians wait in twilight's dream.

Silent watchers, eyes agleam,
Wading through the silver stream.
Moonlit paths where secrets hide,
In their magic, we abide.

They cradle hopes in velvet night,
Lighting paths with gentle light.
Lullabies in softest tones,
Among the stars, their presence shone.

Woven tales of dreams untold,
In the dark, their warmth unfolds.
Every sigh and every plea,
They hold close, their legacy.

As dawn's light begins to break,
From their embrace, we slowly wake.
Yet in our hearts, their whispers remain,
Guardians of dreams, no less, no gain.

Whispers of Celestial Glow

Soft whispers ride the evening breeze,
Stars twinkle softly in silent tease.
Moonlight drapes the world in silver lace,
Awakening dreams in quiet grace.

Night's breath carries secrets untold,
A tapestry woven in threads of gold.
Each shimmer a promise, a wish in flight,
Guiding our hearts through the velvet night.

Dancers in the Night's Embrace

In shadows cast by the pale moonlight,
Figures sway in a graceful flight.
Whispers of laughter, soft as a sigh,
Echo through darkness, like stars on high.

Each turn and twirl, a symphony spun,
Dancing together, two souls become one.
The world fades away, just silence remains,
Lost in the rhythm, where love entertains.

Ethereal Lights Beneath the Stars

Ethereal lights twinkle far and near,
Guiding the lost with warmth and cheer.
Their flicker enchants the watchful eyes,
Whispers of hope beneath endless skies.

In the hush of night, dreams start to glow,
Coloring shadows with a gentle flow.
Each spark a promise of journeys untold,
Awakening hearts, igniting the bold.

Shadows of Enchantment

Shadows dance where the moonlight plays,
A secret world within the maze.
Every corner hides a tale to weave,
In silence, they beckon, inviting to leave.

The air is thick with magic's sweet kiss,
A lingering feeling of unmeasured bliss.
In these darkened depths, bright visions gleam,
Crafting a lattice of wonders and dreams.

Glimmers in Silvered Woods

In the woods where shadows play,
Silent whispers call the day.
Silver leaves in gentle sway,
Nature's heart begins to say.

Glimmers dance upon the ground,
Mossy beds where peace is found.
With each step, soft dreams abound,
In this haven, joy unbound.

Through the trees, a soft breeze flows,
Carrying tales the forest knows.
In the night where magic glows,
Glimmers weave as twilight grows.

Stars peek through the leafy spread,
In the silence, spirits tread.
Underneath the moonlight's bed,
Whispers linger, softly wed.

In the silvered woods we roam,
Finding solace, making home.
Nature's tapestry, we comb,
In this sacred place, we comb.

Moonlit Lullabies and Starlit Dreams

In the hush of the night sky,
Moonlit dreams begin to fly.
Whispers soft as breezes sigh,
Cradled by the stars up high.

Lullabies of shadows play,
Guiding hearts along the way.
In the night, let worries stray,
As the dawn begins to sway.

Each twinkle holds a story near,
Threads of light that draw us here.
In the dark, there's nothing fear,
Starlit dreams will make it clear.

Moonbeams dance on quiet streams,
Waking all our secret dreams.
In the stillness, hope redeems,
Guiding us to love's true themes.

Sleep now, let the night be calm,
Feel the magic, like a balm.
In the stillness, find your psalm,
Moonlit lullabies shall charm.

Mystical Echoes in the Twilight

As the sun begins to yield,
Mystical echoes are revealed.
Twilight wraps the world in grace,
Secrets hidden in this space.

Shadows play on ancient trees,
Carried softly by the breeze.
Whispers dance with softest ease,
In this realm where spirits tease.

Echoes of a bygone age,
Turn the night into a stage.
Every moment sets the page,
For the dusk to disengage.

Colors blend, a painter's muse,
In this world, we cannot lose.
Stories shared are ours to choose,
Stirring depths that we peruse.

In the twilight, magic blooms,
Filling hearts with sweet perfumes.
As the night, the silence looms,
Mystical echoes find their rooms.

Spirits of the Dusk

As the day fades to twilight,
Softly stepping into night.
Spirits whisper, shadows sway,
Wandering souls come out to play.

In the dusk, they come alive,
Echoing what we derive.
Guiding lost hearts to survive,
In the dreams where thoughts contrive.

Breezes carry tales untold,
Ancient stories, brave and bold.
In their dance, we find the gold,
Moments cherished, never cold.

Stars awaken, skies ignite,
Filling hearts with pure delight.
In the calm, our spirits flight,
Dancing 'neath the moon's soft light.

Spirits linger, softly sigh,
In the twilight, never shy.
Holding hands with every high,
In the dusk, we learn to fly.

Veiled Figures in the Night

Shadows dance beneath the trees,
Murmurs blend with the night's cool breeze.
Figures cloaked in mystic grace,
Whispers linger in this secret place.

The moon hangs low, a silver light,
Casting secrets, cloaked in night.
Silent watchers with hidden eyes,
Veiled in dreams, where silence lies.

A gentle rustle in the air,
Hints of stories unaware.
Their laughter echoes, soft and rare,
Haunting tales woven with care.

In twilight's arms, they weave and sway,
Time a ribbon they can't betray.
In the stillness, hearts collide,
Lost and found, they softly glide.

Eclipsed by night, they fade away,
Leaving footprints, astray they play.
Veiled figures in the moon's embrace,
Departing whispers in endless space.

Whispers on the Moon's Edge

Beneath the glow of silver beams,
Secrets sprout within our dreams.
Flutters of wonder in the night,
Whispers dance on edges bright.

Stars align in soft delight,
Guiding hearts through endless flight.
Voices carried from afar,
Echo softly, like a star.

In shadows where the moonlight gleams,
Each sigh holds a thousand themes.
Paths entwined in gentle sway,
Leading lost souls on their way.

Hope ignites like fireflies,
Lighting up the darkened skies.
Every breath a story told,
In silver threads, the night unfolds.

And as the dawn begins to break,
The whispered vows, the love we make.
A tapestry of light and shade,
On moon's edge, our dreams cascade.

Beyond the Veil of Stars

In the realm where wishes soar,
A tapestry of dreams galore.
Each twinkle holds a tale to share,
Glimmers glinted in cosmic air.

Above the echoes of the night,
Fate unfolds in starlit light.
Hearts entwined with threads divine,
Beyond the veil, our hopes align.

Every pulse, a wish sent free,
Drifting through eternity.
Constellations guide the way,
In silence, our spirits sway.

Through endless space, we roam afar,
Chasing shadows of the stars.
In endless dances, we collide,
On cosmic winds, we softly ride.

And when the dawn begins to wake,
The paths of light we start to take.
With every step, the dream's embrace,
Beyond the veil, our sacred space.

The Luminance of Woodland Wishes

In the heart of the forest glade,
Where shadows play and dreams are made.
Luminous flowers paint the floor,
Whispers echo by the door.

Moonlit streams weave through the trees,
Carrying tales on the breeze.
Each soft glow, a wish set free,
In the woodland's tapestry.

Boughs entwined, a sacred dome,
A refuge where our spirits roam.
Celestial sparkles in the night,
Guide the lost toward the light.

Every heartbeat, a promise shared,
In the quiet, no souls are scared.
The forest breathes with gentle sighs,
As shimmering hopes find the skies.

And when the dawn begins to rise,
Softly brightening the darkened skies.
Woodland wishes, softly kissed,
In nature's arms, we still exist.

Veils of Light and Laughter

In the morning's soft embrace,
Laughter dances in the air,
Light weaves through the gentle trees,
Joy unfurls without a care.

Petals glisten with the dew,
Whispered secrets shared aloud,
Days begin with hues so bright,
Nature beckons, dreamers proud.

Sunlight's warmth, a tender kiss,
On the skin, it ignites grace,
Veils of light that beckon bliss,
Every heart finds its own place.

Butterflies flit, laughter calls,
Underneath the azure skies,
Time suspends, and wonder falls,
In this realm, no one denies.

As shadows stretch and whispers fade,
The joy remains, forever weaving,
Veils of light, like dreams displayed,
In the warmth of hearts believing.

Celestial Serenade of the Wilderness

Amidst the trees, the stars convene,
Whispers of the night unfold,
Nature's voice in harmony,
A tale of love and ages told.

Moonlight bathes the silent wood,
Crickets sing of dreams untold,
Each leaf sways in gratitude,
A beauty that will never grow old.

Mountains loom with majesty,
Embracing nights both dark and deep,
Stars compose a symphony,
In this stillness, silence weeps.

Echoes of a time long past,
Flow softly through the tangled ferns,
In the glow of the night's cast,
The spirit of the world returns.

Celestial songs that guide the soul,
Through wilderness, a path to find,
Harmony that makes us whole,
In this embrace, our hearts aligned.

Whirling Stars in a Phantom Glade

In a glade where shadows twirl,
Stars cascade like whispered lore,
Phantoms dance in lunar light,
Mysteries that we explore.

Frosty air, a breath of night,
Echoes of what once had been,
Dreamers linger, hearts ignite,
In the space where time is thin.

Winds of change sweep through the trees,
Carrying tales from afar,
Constellations weave the breeze,
Guiding us beneath the stars.

Veils of mist and silver glow,
A symphony of sights unseen,
What lies hidden, we may know,
In the depths of this serene.

Whirling stars, a cosmic dance,
In a world where phantoms play,
Lose yourself in every chance,
As the night will fade away.

Dreamweavers in the Glow

In the twilight's gentle breath,
Dreamweavers spin tales of light,
Threads of hope and whispers soft,
Crafting visions through the night.

Stars conspire with the moon,
Illuminating dreams we chase,
Every wish a stepping stone,
In a realm of endless grace.

Dancers in the sacred night,
Combining shadows, fates entwined,
Carving paths in glowing hues,
For the seekers, hearts aligned.

Each flicker tells a story,
Of the souls who dare to fly,
Boundless like the sky above,
In the silence, spirits sigh.

Dreamweavers in the twilight's hold,
Guide us with your soft embrace,
Crafting futures, bright and bold,
In the wonder of this place.

Twilight's Radiant Kiss

The sun dips low, hues aglow,
Whispered secrets in the breeze,
Night unfolds her velvet shawl,
As shadows dance among the trees.

Stars awaken, twinkling light,
Embracing dreams in the dark,
Moonbeams paint the world in white,
Nature's canvas, a quiet spark.

Crickets sing their serenade,
While fireflies flicker and play,
A tapestry of joys displayed,
In twilight's gentle ballet.

With every breath, magic stirs,
In the heart of the peaceful night,
Where hope and wonder softly blurs,
In twilight's radiant light.

As darkness wraps its tender hold,
We find solace under the sky,
In this moment, brave and bold,
For in twilight, we learn to fly.

Lanterns of the Nighttime Glade

Deep in the woods where shadows play,
Lanterns flicker, soft and bright,
Guiding spirits lost in the fray,
Through the hush of the velvet night.

Winding paths of ancient lore,
Each glow holds a tale untold,
Whispers of those who've come before,
In the light, their dreams unfold.

Dancing wisps in the forest deep,
A ballet of hopes on the breeze,
Secrets cherished, promises keep,
In the night's gentle tease.

Amidst the trees, a magic rare,
Where hearts unburdened gently roam,
In the glade, we breath the air,
And find ourselves, our true home.

The moon above watches with grace,
On the journey, we're never alone,
In the glade's sweet embrace,
Lanterns brighten, lead us home.

Dreams of the Luminous Wanders

In shadows cast by starlit skies,
Dreamers roam, their spirits free,
With every breath, a wish that flies,
Toward infinity's endless sea.

Whispers weave through the stillness bright,
Echoes of laughter, stories told,
Guided by the soft moonlight,
Each step revealing treasures bold.

Flickers of brilliance, dance of fate,
In the heart of the nocturnal glow,
A symphony of life that waits,
For the brave souls who dare to go.

In the realm where magic flows,
A tapestry of dreams unfurled,
Each heartbeat, an enchanted prose,
Painting the canvas of the world.

So wander forth into the deep,
Seek the wonders yet to be,
For in our dreams, the soul will leap,
And find its place, forever free.

Harmony Beneath the Astral Canopy

Under the vast and twinkling sky,
Harmony sings in soft refrain,
Celestial rhythms, soaring high,
In the night's embrace, none in vain.

Stars align in perfect grace,
A lullaby from realms above,
Guiding whispers, a tender trace,
Binding hearts in timeless love.

Every breath a melody sweet,
With crickets joining in the choir,
Nature and night, a rhythmic beat,
Igniting the soul like fire.

Through silver slivers of moonlight glow,
We find connection, find our way,
In the silence, our spirits flow,
Underneath the starlit sway.

So pause, breathe deep, let go of fears,
For in this space, we come alive,
With harmony cradling the years,
Beneath the stars, we thrive and strive.

Dance of the Spangled Night

Underneath a starry sky,
Whispers of the night do sigh,
Each twinkle tells a tale,
Of dreams that never fail.

Shadows sway in moonlit beams,
As the world drifts into dreams,
Footsteps soft upon the grass,
In this moment, time shall pass.

Laughter echoes through the air,
Joyful hearts without a care,
Spirits rise in pure delight,
As we dance through spangled night.

Galaxies spin, a cosmic waltz,
In the beauty, no faults,
Every heart beat synchronizes,
In the night, magic rises.

In this realm where stardust flows,
Nurtured dreams, forever grows,
As we twirl with wild delight,
Bound together, souls take flight.

Flickers of Fantasy in the Ether

In a realm where wishes play,
Flickers light the hidden way,
Cotton candy clouds appear,
Whispers weave within the sphere.

Chasing shadows on the breeze,
Moments dance among the trees,
Imagination takes its flight,
In the gentle cloak of night.

Dreamers gather, hearts align,
Spinning thoughts like twisted vine,
Every flicker tells a story,
In the dim, we find our glory.

Fading echoes from the past,
Glance at futures set to cast,
Through the ether's misty veil,
Hope and wonder shall prevail.

With each step, a spark ignites,
Magic floats on silver nights,
In this world, illusions blend,
Flickers charm without an end.

Legends of the Night Bloom

In the garden of the dark,
Night blooms whisper, leave their mark,
Petals soft, like velvet skies,
Catching secrets, tender sighs.

Moonlight swathes each fragrant hue,
As the stars beckon anew,
Legends stir upon the breeze,
Stories dance in whispered leaves.

Every blossom, a tale unfolds,
Of daring dreams and hearts of gold,
In the twilight, shadows play,
As night blooms guide the way.

Nature's canvas painted bright,
In the hush of velvet night,
With each breath, the magic flows,
In the dark, the beauty grows.

Awakened spirits, spirits roam,
In the night, we find our home,
With the bloom beneath the skies,
Legends live, and never die.

Enchanted Paths to the Moon's Caress

Winding trails through silver light,
Call to hearts in tranquil night,
Steps will lead to wonder's door,
Where the moonlight whispers more.

With each turn, the magic plays,
Lighting up forgotten ways,
Every shadow we embrace,
In the glow of moon's soft face.

Echoes of a distant song,
Guide us gently, lead us long,
On enchanted paths we tread,
Chasing dreams, where hope has led.

Celestial guides in the sky,
Nurturing as we glide by,
In the stillness, time does pause,
Underneath the moon's sweet cause.

With every promise, hearts will dance,
On this path, we take a chance,
In the magic's warm embrace,
Find the moon's eternal grace.

Beneath the Shimmering Canopy

Whispers dance on twilight breeze,
Leaves flutter like secrets told.
Stars blink down, the night's soft tease,
In shadows where dreams unfold.

Moonlight bathes the forest floor,
A quilt of silver, soft and bright.
Creatures stir and softly soar,
Awakening in the gentle night.

Branches arch like ancient walls,
Guardians of the night's embrace.
Nature's symphony softly calls,
Inviting all to join the chase.

A hush descends, the world in tune,
With crickets chirping, soft and low.
Beneath the shimmering moon,
Where magic sways, and rivers flow.

In this realm, time feels so sweet,
Each moment stretches, laced with grace.
A tranquil heart, a rhythmic beat,
Beneath the trees, in this sacred space.

Enigmas of the Moonlit Glade

In the glade where shadows play,
Mysteries linger in the night.
Softly glimmers the silver ray,
Illuminating paths of light.

Whispers echo among the leaves,
Secrets shrouded in the dark.
Nature weaves its web and weaves,
A tapestry, a whispered spark.

Dewdrops glisten on the grass,
Like jewels dropped from heaven's chest.
In quietude, the moments pass,
Each heartbeat finds its perfect rest.

Allure of night enfolds the air,
With every step, a tale untold.
In this dreamscape, we ensnare,
The enigma of the moonlight bold.

As starlight twinkles overhead,
We lose ourselves in night's caress.
In the glade, our spirits spread,
Enigmas wrapped in starlit dress.

Silhouettes of Magic at Dusk

When the sun sinks low and shy,
Colors blend in soft farewell.
Shadows dance as night draws nigh,
In the dusk, enchantments dwell.

Figures flicker, fleeting sights,
Casting dreams on fading light.
In this hour, the magic ignites,
Weaving tales of sheer delight.

Crisp air teems with silent songs,
Unseen threads of twilight weave.
In the dark, where magic throngs,
All that's lost begins to grieve.

With every breath, the essence sways,
Drifting whispers on the chill.
In the dusk, the heart's ablaze,
As mysteries our senses fill.

In silhouettes against the sky,
All that lingers, a gentle trust.
Magic whispers soft and sly,
At dusk's embrace, in twilight's rust.

Celestial Revelry in Woodland Shadows

In woodland depths, the stars align,
A cosmic dance in subtle light.
Echoes of a grand design,
Celebrate the nature's night.

Shadows sway with joyous grace,
As creatures gather, hearts entwined.
In this realm, time finds its pace,
Celestial rhythms intertwined.

The moon unfolds her silken gown,
Casting dreams upon the trail.
Whispers of the night renown,
Breathe life into the fairy tale.

Beneath the trees, we lose our way,
In revelry of starry schemes.
In the shadows, come what may,
We weave together our wild dreams.

The night ignites with laughter bright,
As nature's chorus fills the air.
Celestial magic, pure delight,
In woodland shadows, free from care.

Spirits at the Glistening Tide

Whispers rise where waters gleam,
Ghostly forms in moonlit beam.
Waves that dance on silver light,
Call the souls to take their flight.

Footprints fade on sandy shore,
Echoes of the tales of yore.
Softly laughter fills the air,
As the spirits wander there.

Crimson hues at dusk descend,
Nature's beauty never ends.
Breezes carry whispered sighs,
Underneath the twilight skies.

In the dark, the tides conspire,
To ignite the heart's desire.
From the depths, they softly glide,
Joining hands with the glistening tide.

Reflections in the Celestial Pool

Stars adorn the silent night,
Shimmering in water's bite.
Every ripple holds a dream,
Mirrored visions softly gleam.

Moonlight bathes the tranquil shore,
Secrets whispered evermore.
In the depths, the stillness keeps,
Ancient tales as silence weeps.

Beneath the surface, worlds collide,
In this haven, hearts confide.
Echoes of the past resound,
In this sacred space, we're found.

Glimmers flicker, shadows sway,
In the night, they drift away.
Water's edge invites us near,
To face all that we hold dear.

Oracles of the Night

Underneath the blanket dark,
Whispers spark a hidden arc.
Stars align in woven threads,
Carrying the fates we dread.

Voices rise on midnight's breath,
Foretelling dreams and whispered death.
Circles drawn in ancient stone,
Echo prophecies alone.

The moon reflects our deepest fears,
As shadows dance and disappear.
Silent watchers from above,
Guide us with their ancient love.

In the stillness, answers flow,
Revealing truths we long to know.
With each gaze, the night unfolds,
A tapestry of tales retold.

Chiaroscuro Dreams of the Enchanted

Light and shadow intertwine,
In a world both yours and mine.
Dreams arise from dusky hues,
Where enchantment softly brews.

Through the forest, echoes play,
Mysterious realms lead the way.
Golden glimmers pierce the veil,
To unveil the hidden trail.

Mirrored lakes reflect our hopes,
In the dark, our spirit copes.
Each step taken, visions bloom,
In the night, dispelling gloom.

Touch the light, embrace the shade,
In this dance, we're unafraid.
Chiaroscuro holds the key,
To the magic we will see.

Trace of Wings in Moonlight

In the hush of night's embrace,
A silhouette takes flight,
Wings like whispers, soft and light,
Tracing dreams in moonlit space.

Silver beams through branches weave,
Guiding the wayward soul,
With each flutter, fragments whole,
In the night, we dare believe.

Stars above begin to twine,
As shadows dance on silent ground,
Echoes of a love once found,
In the heart where hopes align.

A gentle breeze now sways the trees,
Inviting memories to play,
As dawn threatens to decay,
The magic found within the leaves.

In twilight's grasp, the world holds tight,
To fleeting moments, lost and rare,
Yet in dreams, they linger there,
Forever captured by the night.

Sorrows and Joys of the Night

In shadows deep, where secrets lie,
A symphony of hearts will break,
Each tear that falls, a silent ache,
Yet in the dark, we learn to fly.

Whispers softly brush the ground,
With every sigh, a story told,
A tapestry in silver and gold,
In sorrows sweet, joy can be found.

The moon, a guardian in the void,
Watches over the lost and meek,
Guiding the dreams that softly speak,
To kindred spirits, once destroyed.

A tapestry of night's embrace,
Where laughter mingles with the tears,
And through the pain, love reappears,
In every shadow, joy finds space.

With every heartbeat, life resumes,
Embracing both the dark and light,
A dance of souls, a timeless rite,
In the night's sweet, fragrant blooms.

The Celestial Mosaic of Shadows

In the galaxy of dreams we float,
Each star a piece of whispered light,
Mosaics built with day and night,
In colors deep, they gently bloat.

Shadows waltz through the cosmic haze,
Where planets hum their ancient tunes,
And hope abounds like swirling moons,
Awakening in the softest ways.

A tapestry of cosmic fate,
Threads of silver, dark and bright,
Unearth the heart's forgotten light,
In harmony, we weave, not wait.

In the arms of sleep, we wander far,
Through galaxies, we roam and dream,
In every shadow, every beam,
A universe contained in a star.

Together we'll explore the night,
With every heartbeat, every sigh,
As the shadows soar and fly,
In celestial skies, our spirits flight.

Waltz of the Ethereal Creatures

In twilight's glow, they start their dance,
Ethereal beings, light as air,
With fluttering grace, they sway and share,
A cosmic rhythm, a love's romance.

Moonbeams shower down with grace,
Illuminating each delicate wing,
In the night, their voices sing,
A serenade in the starlit space.

Each creature spins a tale untold,
Of wonders vast and dreams unbound,
In the silence, they're profound,
In the depths of night, they brave, bold.

Through shadows thick and whispers light,
Together they weave a dreamlike web,
With every heartbeat, every ebb,
In darkness, they find pure delight.

A carousel of moments shared,
Where joy and grace entwine as one,
In the dance of night, we're never done,
In the waltz of spirits, all are cared.

Whispers of the Night Sky

The moon hangs low, a watchful eye,
Its silvery beams, softly sigh.
Stars twinkle with tales untold,
In the vast expanse, mysteries unfold.

Clouds drift like dreams in the night,
Carrying whispers, a gentle flight.
The cosmos hums a lullaby sweet,
Guiding the lost on their celestial feet.

Silhouettes dance on the velvet dark,
Each flicker of light, a hidden spark.
In shadows cast by the heavenly glow,
Wonders of the universe begin to flow.

Fading echoes of sunlight's grace,
In twilight's arms, we find our place.
The night unfolds its secrets wide,
With every breath, we coincide.

Dreams take flight on starlit streams,
As we wander through inky seams.
In whispers of the night, we find,
Connection deep within our mind.

Murmurs of the Enchanted Breeze

In the hush of woods, a soft caress,
Whispers glide through trees, they bless.
The leaves respond in a gentle sway,
Telling stories of the day.

Petals flutter in fragrant air,
While secrets linger, free from care.
Each gust carries a soothing song,
Nature's orchestra, not loud, but strong.

Rippling streams add their serenade,
In harmony with the twilight's fade.
The murmurs of twilight weave spells bright,
Illuminating the approaching night.

With every breath, the world feels new,
Embraced in magic, a wondrous view.
The essence of dusk, a blessing shared,
In every whisper, a spirit bared.

As shadows deepen, the breeze still sings,
Of love and loss, of fleeting things.
In its embrace, we find our peace,
As dreams and reality softly crease.

Starlit Secrets of the Hallowed Grove

Beneath the canopy, shadows dance,
In the heart of night, we twirl in trance.
Each branch and leaf, a secret kept,
While ancient roots in silence wept.

Soft glimmers break the inky dome,
Each star above feels like home.
In this grove where time stands still,
Nature's breath flows with gentle will.

Whispers of spirits, the trees confide,
Tales of wonder and love that bide.
The air is thick with history old,
In every heartbeat, a story told.

Luminous orbs guide our way,
In their light, shadows choose to sway.
Every rustle holds a promise bright,
In the hallowed grove under starlit light.

As we wander through this sacred place,
Each step reveals a hidden grace.
With open hearts, we listen keen,
To the starlit secrets, soft and serene.

Serenade of the Wandering Spirits

In moonlit dreams, the spirits roam,
Carrying whispers from their home.
They dance on breezes, light as air,
Leaving traces of love and care.

Echoes of laughter, tales of old,
Entwined in silver, dusted gold.
Their voices blend with the nightingale,
A serenade, a mystical trail.

Wandering paths, where shadows play,
In every corner, the night holds sway.
They gather close, a celestial choir,
Sparkling hopes, igniting desire.

In the stillness, they weave their song,
A melody where spirits belong.
With every note, hearts intertwine,
In the serenade, spirits align.

As dawn approaches, they start to fade,
But their whispers linger, a soft cascade.
In memories held, they forever twine,
Wandering spirits, in rhythm divine.

Luminescent Secrets of the Forest

In shadows deep where secrets dwell,
The forest glows with tales to tell.
A dance of light, a whispering breeze,
Amongst the leaves, as time does freeze.

Mossy paths where dreams align,
Each step reveals a hidden sign.
Creatures small with glistening eyes,
Guarding truths beneath the skies.

Flickering fireflies weave the night,
Casting spells of soft delight.
Ancient trees with stories old,
Hold mysteries that still unfold.

Through twisted roots and emerald shade,
The magic swirls, the memories fade.
In silence, secrets softly grow,
Whispered promises of long ago.

With every breath, the forest sighs,
Echoing life in muted cries.
In luminescent realms, we find,
The heart of nature, intertwined.

Chasing Whispers of the Night

Beneath the stars, the shadows roam,
In velvet darkness, we find home.
Each whispered breeze, a tale from far,
Guiding the way like a northern star.

Moonlight dances on silver streams,
Colors fade into twilight dreams.
Footsteps hush on the forest floor,
As echoes linger, forevermore.

With every sigh, the night unfolds,
Stories of lovers and legends told.
Stars above in their watchful gaze,
Illuminate the night's soft maze.

Owls call softly, a secret's plea,
In the stillness, we feel the free.
Chasing whispers on the night air,
Discovering wonders that linger there.

Each heartbeat syncs with nature's song,
In the night, where we belong.
As dreams entwine with silence clear,
We chase the whispers, drawing near.

Twilight's Gentle Breath

As daylight fades to twilight's glow,
A tender breeze begins to flow.
In shades of purple, gold, and blue,
The world transforms, begins anew.

Crickets chirp as night descends,
Nature's lullaby, the heart mends.
Softly wrap in dusk's embrace,
Time slows down in this sacred space.

Each fleeting moment, a breath of grace,
Painting shadows on nature's face.
This gentle breath, a calming sigh,
Inviting dreams as stars drift by.

In twilight's hold, we find our peace,
A whispered promise, sweet release.
With every color, the heart's delight,
Awakens here in soft twilight.

Let go of worries, let silence reign,
In tranquil moments, escape the strain.
As twilight dances through the air,
A gentle breath, forever rare.

Radiant Beings of the Undergrowth

In hidden realms where wonders gleam,
Radiant beings dance through dreams.
With jeweled wings and voices sweet,
They weave a magic, pure and neat.

Among the ferns, they twist and sway,
In whispered tones, they greet the day.
With every flutter, secrets shared,
A world enchanting, love declared.

In tiny spaces, life abounds,
Their vibrant hues in silence found.
The undergrowth, a tapestry,
Of wonders rare for all to see.

A harmony of nature's song,
Where delicate and bold belong.
With radiant hearts that light the way,
In shadows deep, they brightly play.

As dusk descends, their glow ignites,
Transforming paths with gentle lights.
In the underbrush, all creatures thrive,
Radiant beings, so alive.

Echoes of Lanterned Magic

In twilight's glow, the lanterns sway,
Casting whispers upon the bay.
Stars awaken from their sleep,
Painting secrets, rich and deep.

Winds carry tales from years gone by,
Softly echoing the night sky.
Each light a wish, a dream, a spark,
Dancing gently in the dark.

A flickering glow on waters wide,
Reflections of a world inside.
Where shadows play and spirits roam,
In this magic, we find home.

The fireflies join in the rhyme,
Marking fleeting moments in time.
As laughter echoes through the night,
Illuminating pure delight.

In lantern's glow, hopes intertwine,
A tapestry of light divine.
Let your heart take flight and soar,
As echoes call forevermore.

Shadows of the Dreamweaver's Realm

In the realm where dreams reside,
Shadows dance, and spirits glide.
Whispers weave through silence deep,
Cradling secrets, lost in sleep.

A silver mist wraps the trees,
Carrying tales whispered on the breeze.
Where wishes come and fears dissolve,
In a mystery, we evolve.

Softly glows the moonlight pale,
Guiding wanderers with its trail.
As shadows bloom in midnight's grasp,
With each heartbeat, our dreams clasp.

The Dreamweaver spins threads of gold,
Crafting visions both brave and bold.
In this space, we dare to fly,
Unraveling truths beneath the sky.

In the harmony of night's embrace,
Shadows reveal their gentle grace.
Let dreams linger, let them thrive,
In the realm where we are alive.

Interplay of Radiance and Shade

In morning's blush, shadows retreat,
As sunlight dances, soft and sweet.
Radiance spills on earth below,
Painting landscapes, rich in glow.

Dappled light through trees will play,
Creating patterns, come what may.
Branches sway to nature's tune,
While whispers hum beneath the moon.

Clouds drift overhead, a soft embrace,
Shifting moments, a gentle grace.
In twilight's hue, the world transforms,
As night unveils its soothing forms.

The stars emerge, their light anew,
Stitching darkness with threads of blue.
In this dance of light and shade,
Beauty flourishes, unafraid.

From dawn till dusk, let colors sing,
In every heart, the joys they bring.
For in the interplay, we find,
The light and dark, forever twined.

Night's Tapestry Woven with Lights

The night unfolds a hidden thread,
With stars like jewels, softly spread.
A tapestry of dreams takes flight,
In the quiet arms of night.

Constellations weave ancient tales,
Carried by the starlit gales.
Each flicker, a story shared,
In the celestial quilt, prepared.

Moonbeams dance on rivers wide,
Guiding hearts with gentle pride.
As shadows stroll through whispered sighs,
The night reveals its sweet disguise.

Crickets sing a lullaby,
As dreams unfurl and softly fly.
A canvas brushed with twilight's hue,
In every heart, a spark anew.

Under the blanket of the sky,
Woven lights make wishes fly.
In night's embrace, we find our peace,
As the magic of dreams will never cease.

Luminous Dancers of the Night

Stars twinkle bright in the dark,
They weave their tales in golden arcs.
With whispers low, they sway and spin,
Night's gentle waltz, the magic within.

Moonlight drapes the earth like silk,
Illuminating dreams and thoughts to milk.
The sky becomes their gleaming stage,
As night unfolds, they dance and engage.

Each flicker tells a story untold,
Of hidden wishes and hopes of old.
In twilight's arms, they find their grace,
With every movement, they carve their space.

With laughter soft, they toss their light,
In harmony with the restful night.
The cosmos sings, a symphony rare,
As luminous dancers paint the air.

And when dawn creeps with its gentle yawn,
The dancers fade, till the break of dawn.
Yet in our hearts, their glow will stay,
Guiding us through night's shadowed play.

Ethereal Glow of Hidden Realms

Beyond the veil where shadows drift,
Lies a world where dreams are swift.
An ethereal glow bathes the land,
Inviting hearts to take a stand.

Glimmers of magic in every glance,
Creatures of night lead us to dance.
With whispers soft, they call our names,
In hidden realms where nothing's the same.

Each ray of light holds secrets dear,
Shimmering softly, soothing our fear.
In the twilight, we find our way,
Through ethereal glow, we dare to stay.

Memories woven in silver threads,
With every heartbeat, the moment spreads.
Together we journey, hand in hand,
In a realm where wonders expand.

Ethereal glow, a guiding light,
Illuminating paths throughout the night.
With every step, our spirits soar,
As hidden realms reveal their door.

The Sylvan Serenade at Dusk

Woodlands hush as twilight falls,
Echoing softly the evening calls.
Leaves rustle gently, a lulled refrain,
In the sylvan serenade, life gains.

Crickets chirp their rhythmic tune,
Filling the air beneath the moon.
With shadows long and whispers deep,
The forest awakens from its sleep.

Birds retreat to their hidden nest,
As twilight blankets the day's quest.
Stars peek through the foliage green,
In this serene space, calm and unseen.

The breeze carries secrets of the night,
As fireflies dance, aglow with light.
Nature's chorus, a timeless sound,
In the sylvan serenade, peace is found.

As darkness draws the curtain near,
The world transforms, a tapestry clear.
In sylvan arms, we gently sway,
Lost in the serenade's soft play.

Elusive Luminaries of the Gloaming

As dusk descends, the shadows blend,
Elusive luminaries appear and send.
Whispers of light in the fading glow,
They dance between the realms below.

Glimpses bright, like fleeting dreams,
Sparkling softly in silver streams.
They weave their magic in the air,
Elusive forms that shimmer and dare.

In twilight's cloak, they twirl and spin,
A cosmic ballet that draws us in.
Guiding our hearts with gentle grace,
These luminaries fill the space.

With colors rich, beyond our sight,
They teach us wonder in the night.
Elusive stars that come alive,
In gloaming's embrace, we revive.

As the world quiets with soft sighs,
We breathe deep and lift our eyes.
For in the gloaming, dreams are born,
Elusive luminaries greet each dawn.

Luminary Secrets in the Mist

In the hush of dawn's first light,
Shadows whisper tales of night.
Veils of fog, like secrets spun,
Hide the dreams of everyone.

Stars still glimmer in the gray,
Fleeting glances drift away.
Mysteries in every sigh,
Echo softly as they fly.

Winds of fate weave through the trees,
Carrying ancient melodies.
Nature hums a spectral tune,
Cradled softly by the moon.

Footprints linger on the ground,
Silent stories all around.
In the misty twilight's breath,
Life awakens, dances with death.

Beneath the clouds, a truth will bloom,
Shattering the self-made gloom.
In the stillness, hearts align,
Revealing secrets, so divine.

Enchanted Dances on the Horizon

From the edge of day, they twirl,
Colors collide, a vivid swirl.
Horizons beckon with their grace,
Dancing shadows interlace.

Beneath the arch of twilight sky,
Whispers of the past drift by.
Footsteps tracing stardust lines,
Echoes etched in ancient signs.

Nightfall brings its soothing song,
Melodies where spirits throng.
In the moonlight, dreams take flight,
Creating magic of the night.

Breezes carry laughter's sound,
As enchanted hearts abound.
Waltzing through the velvet air,
In this realm, love's everywhere.

With each spin, a story's told,
In the dark, see wonders unfold.
The horizon glows with hope and cheer,
Forever captured, ever near.

Guardians of the Midnight Realm

In shadows deep, with watchful eyes,
Silent sentinels, they rise.
Guarding secrets cloaked in night,
Safeguarding dreams with all their might.

Wings of darkness, soft and wide,
With every heartbeat, they glide.
Whispers echo on the breeze,
Bringing warmth, with such ease.

Ancient voices call like prayer,
Caring for all dreams laid bare.
In the stillness, they confide,
Illusions fade, the truth won't hide.

With starlit paths and moonbeam trails,
They weave enchantment, told in tales.
Spirits dance upon the ground,
In their embrace, warmth is found.

Guardians true of every heart,
Supporting souls from worlds apart.
In midnight's glow, find your peace,
Through their watch, your fears release.

Gossamer Wings on a Lunar Night

In silver glow, the night unfolds,
Gossamer wings, a sight to behold.
Fluttering softly through the air,
Wonders woven with such care.

Moonlight dances on each thread,
With dreams of hopes that lie ahead.
Whispers carry tales from afar,
Guiding hearts like a shooting star.

Beneath the canopy of dark,
Magic waits for that first spark.
Each flutter sings of forgotten lore,
Transporting souls to distant shores.

Bathed in light, they shimmer bright,
Life's fragile threads, a wondrous sight.
Floating gently with the breeze,
A moment's peace, a heart's ease.

In the embrace of shadows, they glide,
Carrying hopes that never hide.
Gossamer dreams take their flight,
On this sweet, enchanting night.

Veiled Wonders of the Nocturnal Wood

In the quiet grove where shadows play,
Moonlight whispers secrets of the day.
Ancient trees bend low and sigh,
While owls serenade the velvet sky.

Silken threads of mist weave through the night,
Dancing softly in the pale starlight.
Faint footsteps echo on the forest floor,
As dreams entwine with twilight's lore.

A silver brook sings a timeless tune,
Casting ripples that glimmer like the moon.
Fireflies flicker, tiny lanterns aglow,
Guiding lost wanderers where none may go.

Underneath the boughs so thick and wide,
Magic lingers, secrets never hide.
Each rustle of leaves tells tales untold,
Of love and loss in the woods of old.

Veiled wonders wait for those who seek,
In the hush where the ancient echoes speak.
Embrace the night, let your spirit roam,
In the nocturnal wood, find your way home.

The Enchanted Wisp's Journey

Through the glade where shadows dance,
A wisp of light twirls, lost in a trance.
Glimmers of hope in the darkest night,
Leading the way with radiant flight.

Over hills draped in softest moss,
Promises whisper, no worries or loss.
With every flicker, tales arise,
Of dreams and wishes beneath the skies.

Past the brambles and the twisted trees,
The wisp beckons with a gentle breeze.
Carrying magic on its delicate glow,
Guiding the heart where few dare to go.

A mirror of stars in the river's seam,
Reflecting the essence of a secret dream.
Echoes of laughter, of joy and of tears,
Dance through the night, embracing our fears.

So follow the light where shadows occur,
The enchanted wisp's journey will stir.
Illuminating paths never thought found,
In the heart of the night, magic is crowned.

Secrets in the Moonlit Glade

Beneath the silver veil of night,
Secrets whisper in the soft moonlight.
Crickets serenade the sleeping earth,
Tales of wonder, echoes of birth.

Ancient stones hold wisdom deep,
Guarding the dreams that the forest keeps.
Branches sway, casting shadows that weave,
Inviting all wanderers to believe.

In the heart of the glade, a fire burns bright,
Illuminating faces, a mystical sight.
The laughter of friends dances on air,
Invoking the magic that fuels their care.

As night draws close and stars appear,
The glade awakens, embracing the near.
With every heartbeat, a story unfolds,
In the tapestry of night, the truth is told.

So linger awhile where the moonlight sways,
Unravel the secrets in divine arrays.
In the moonlit glade where spirits play free,
Find the magic and let your heart be.

A Dance of Light and Shadows

When the sun dips low and night takes hold,
Shadows emerge; their stories unfold.
A dance begins, a waltz so rare,
Of light entwined with the evening air.

Flickers of flame against the dusky hue,
Guiding the travelers, both old and new.
Each step they take is a rhythmic embrace,
In the theater of night where time finds its pace.

Whispers of secrets shared by the trees,
Rustle and shimmer, akin to soft breeze.
In the canvas of twilight, all is unveiled,
As the stars twinkle, and darkness paled.

With each heartbeat, the dance swirls around,
A symphony woven from silence profound.
In shadows and light, we lose all our fears,
Embracing the magic that lingers for years.

So take my hand in this nocturnal flight,
Together we'll twirl in the arms of the night.
For in the ballet of dark and the bright,
Awaits a world where we find pure delight.

Threads of Magic in the Stillness

In the quiet night, whispers weave,
Gentle dreams on spider's threads,
Stars blink softly, secrets leave,
Where silence sleeps, the heart treads.

Fingers trace the moonlit air,
Each twinkle tells a story bright,
Nature's pulse, a tender care,
In stillness lies the world's delight.

Among the shadows, magic glows,
Enchanting souls to drift and sway,
Invisible dance that nature shows,
Inviting all to softly play.

Winds whisper low, a lullaby,
Serenading thoughts once lost,
Embraced by night, the spirits fly,
To find again what's worth the cost.

Threads of magic, softly spun,
In twilight's grasp, we find our way,
Where all begins, and time is none,
In the stillness, forever stay.

The Glow of Forever Whispers

Beyond the hills, a soft light glows,
A hint of warmth in the twilight's hush,
Where every heartache gently flows,
And echoes linger in the rush.

Whispers of ages drift on air,
Carrying tales both bold and bright,
In shadows deep, we lay our care,
Finding solace in the night.

Hope is a flame, flickering low,
Yet in its glow, the night will sing,
Of moments caught in time's sweet flow,
A dance of dreams that life can bring.

Through the silence, voices rise,
Harmonies shared beneath the stars,
A tapestry of our replies,
Stitched together, healing scars.

In every heartbeat, stories dwell,
The glow of forever, a gentle guide,
In sacred whispers, we can tell,
The light within that won't subside.

Moonlit Revelries in the Wild

Beneath the moon's soft silver gaze,
Wildflowers dance in the evening breeze,
Mysteries wrap the nocturnal maze,
As shadows sway among the trees.

Laughter spills like bubbling brooks,
A chorus of nature, wild and free,
In hidden glades, in secret nooks,
Night's revelry calls, come play with me.

Fireflies twinkle, a starry raid,
Each flicker a delight in the dark,
In this wild realm, worries fade,
With every heartbeat, we leave our mark.

Echoes of joy in the midnight air,
Strummed by breezes, a soft refrain,
Captured in moonlight's tender care,
Where wild souls come to bask in gain.

Under the stars, we roam untamed,
Whispers of freedom in every sound,
In moonlit revelries, we're unclaimed,
In the wild's embrace, forever found.

Radiance of the Enchanted Vale

In the valley where dreams unfold,
Golden hues kiss the dawn's embrace,
A tale of magic, quietly told,
In each petal's dance, there lies grace.

Mountains loom with a silent pride,
Guardians of whispers, ancient and wise,
Reflecting the calm of the river's glide,
Beneath the vast and limitless skies.

Each sunrise brings a vibrant hue,
Awakening flowers in joyful cheer,
In this vale, life's wonders brew,
Inviting hearts to draw near.

Breezes carry laughter on the wind,
Nature's symphony, a gentle song,
In the vale, all sorrows rescind,
Where every soul can truly belong.

With every heartbeat, the magic grows,
In the enchanted vale, we stay,
Where love and light forever flows,
Radiance brightens each passing day.

Beneath the Celestial Veil's Glow

Beneath the stars, where silence breathes,
A dance of light in gentle weave.
Whispers of night call out our names,
While dreams awake, igniting flames.

The moon hangs low, a silver crown,
Casting its glow on sleepy town.
Each twinkle tells a tale untold,
Of hearts entwined and secrets bold.

The sky unfolds in endless swirls,
Where ancient truths begin to whirls.
Lost among constellations bright,
We find our way in starry night.

With every sigh, the cosmos breathes,
In every moment, magic weaves.
Beneath this veil, we dance and sway,
Embraced by night, we drift away.

A journey starts with playful spark,
Amidst the dreams that light the dark.
In the celestial glow we'd roam,
With love as our eternal home.

The Mystique of Wandering Spirits

Beyond the veil, where shadows beckon,
Whispers dance and light can reckon.
Wandering spirits roam the night,
Guided by the faintest light.

In moonlit woods, where echoes play,
They tell of stories lost in grey.
Each rustle speaks of timeless lore,
Of love and loss forever more.

Their laughter rings like silver chimes,
Echoing through forgotten times.
In every breeze a secret sigh,
From souls that wander, never die.

They wander far, yet linger near,
In every heartbeat, feel them here.
The mystique of spirits, so alive,
In every moment, they survive.

And as the dawn begins to break,
The night yields gently, dreams must wake.
Yet in our hearts, we hold them tight,
These wandering souls, our guiding light.

Chasing Shadows in Dream's Embrace

In twilight's hush, where dreams take flight,
We chase the shadows, dance in light.
With whispered thoughts, our fates entwined,
In realms of wonder, souls aligned.

Each step a rhythm, soft and slow,
The world around begins to glow.
In dream's embrace, we find our way,
Through winds of fate, come what may.

The shadows whisper secrets deep,
In silent patterns, memories seep.
We float on clouds of endless schemes,
Awake in night, yet lost in dreams.

As dawn approaches, light will rise,
Yet still the dream will hold its prize.
In every shadow, hope remains,
A dance of love where nothing wanes.

So let us chase the fading night,
With hearts alight in pure delight.
For in the shadows, we may find,
A world of wonders, intertwined.

Starlight's Caress on Leafy Bough

Beneath the branches, softly swaying,
Where fireflies dance and night is playing.
Starlight's touch on leafy bough,
Whispers of magic, here and now.

With every rustle, secrets flow,
In twilight's arms, the wonders grow.
The moon bestows a silver kiss,
On nature's heart, a gentle bliss.

Each leaf aglow with luminous grace,
Illuminates this sacred space.
In quiet moments, time stands still,
As starlight dreams with earthly will.

In whispered tones, the night unfolds,
A tapestry of tales retold.
Together cradled in this light,
We find our peace, our soul's delight.

So linger long beneath the tree,
Where starlit whispers set us free.
In nature's arms, we're meant to grow,
Forever held in starlight's glow.

Ethereal Glimmers at Dusk

In twilight's gentle sigh, they dance,
Fleeting whispers, a night's romance.
Stars awaken in the velvet sky,
Casting secrets as they flicker by.

Softly fading, the day's last glow,
Dreams take flight in the evening's flow.
Shadows lengthen, the world grows still,
Embracing night with a quiet thrill.

Mysterious hues paint the horizon,
A canvas where twilight's brush has shone.
Luminous orbs in a celestial play,
Guide lost souls on their wayward way.

Whispers of magic fill the air,
Nature holds tales beyond compare.
Terrene and ether entwine their fate,
In the dusk's embrace, we patiently wait.

Ethereal glimmers, a wondrous sight,
Savoring peace in the heart of night.
For every sparkle that softly beams,
Holds the essence of our deepest dreams.

The Sorcery of Shimmering Light

In the forest's grasp, a secret gleams,
Where starlit shadows weave through dreams.
Golden rays on emerald leaves,
Nature's magic, the heart believes.

Dewdrops glisten like diamonds rare,
Whispering tales of the wondrous fair.
Beams of sunlight filter through the trees,
Carrying laughter on the softest breeze.

Glimmers of hope in the morning air,
Each moment crafted with loving care.
The sorcery lies in the light's embrace,
A dance of warmth that time won't erase.

As twilight beckons with pastel hues,
Nightfall wraps the world in blues.
Yet still the glimmer holds its sway,
Binding the night in a gentle play.

With every flicker, a story unfurls,
Of whispered dreams in the waking worlds.
The sorcery of shimmering light,
A spell cast gently, enchanting the night.

Spirits of the Shimmering Grove

In the hush of dusk, the spirits rise,
Dancing softly beneath starry skies.
Through whispering leaves, they glide with grace,
Guardians of nature, they find their place.

Luminescent forms in a tranquil air,
Breath of magic, delicate and rare.
They weave through branches, embrace the night,
Fleeting voices in the moon's soft light.

Dreamlike figures, the ancient kind,
Echoing stories lost to time behind.
Their laughter rings like a gentle chime,
Inviting all to take a step sublime.

Every shadow holds a tale to tell,
Secrets that cast a timeless spell.
The shimmering grove, a haven bright,
Where spirits whisper in heart's delight.

So wander softly where the wild things grow,
Feel the enchantment, let your spirit flow.
In the grove's embrace, find your way home,
With spirits dancing, we're never alone.

Enchantment in the Stillness of Night

Beneath the moon's watchful eye we gaze,
Where dreams awaken in softest haze.
Silent echoes of the world unwind,
Whispers of magic, in shadows, entwined.

Stars blanket the vastness, twinkling bright,
Guided by love, in the still of the night.
Each moment a treasure, a fleeting spark,
Illuminating paths through the deepening dark.

Shadows stretch long, as time slips away,
Holding the stories of night and day.
The heart finds solace in rhythms slow,
In breaths of wonder, where memories flow.

Like soft lullabies, the night softly hums,
A chorus of nature, the stillness becomes.
In every heartbeat, a promise unfolds,
Enchantment awaits in the tales yet untold.

So linger awhile in the midnight's embrace,
Let your spirit dance, find your own space.
For in this stillness, with whispers alight,
We find our magic, in the depth of night.

Echoes of Light on Leafy Paths

Whispers of leaves dance in the air,
Sunlight filters through, gentle and rare.
Every step taken in shadow and gleam,
Nature's own magic, a tranquil dream.

Birdsong weaves tales in the green embrace,
Each echoing note finds its rightful place.
Among the tall trees, where secrets abide,
Footprints of wanderers, nature's own guide.

Gentle breezes carry stories untold,
Of moments in silence, both tender and bold.
Paths woven in sunlight, in shade intertwined,
Echoes of light where the heart is aligned.

Colors of seasons, a painter's delight,
Each hue a memory, a fleeting sight.
A canvas of life, painted clear and bright,
Echoes of light on leafy paths ignite.

In this sacred space, time slows its pace,
Every heartbeat matches the forest's grace.
With echoes of light, we find our own way,
In leafy paths, where we long to stay.

Luminescent Journeys Through Night

Stars sprinkle silver on the midnight blue,
Whispers of peace in the cool night dew.
Each step a promise, each breath a sigh,
Luminescent journeys beneath the sky.

Moonlit reflections dance on the stream,
Guiding lost souls in a silvery dream.
With each gentle heartbeat, the night unfolds,
Stories of wanderers, both young and old.

Patterns of shadows in soft twilight,
Leading us onward, through the velvet night.
A chorus of crickets sings sweet and clear,
Welcoming travelers who linger near.

Branches sway gently, a soft lullaby,
As fireflies flicker, like stars on high.
The world in this moment feels endlessly bright,
In luminescent journeys, we find our light.

With every heartbeat, we're guided along,
In the embrace of night, we find where we belong.
As dreams intertwine with the deep velvet sky,
Luminescent journeys where hearts learn to fly.

Dreams Woven in Warden Trees

Among the tall giants, dreams softly sway,
Whispers of hope in the light of day.
Threads of the future with roots of the past,
In warden trees' embrace, our visions are cast.

Leaves tell their stories in hues of the dawn,
Each gentle rustle, a sweet, soothing song.
A tapestry woven from moments we share,
In the shade of the trees, we breathe in the air.

Time intertwines in a delicate dance,
Each sigh of the forest, a second chance.
Dreams bloom like flowers from branches above,
In warden trees' arms, we find our love.

The heart of the forest sings quiet and low,
Casting its magic, letting us grow.
As we wander through shadows, the sunlight breaks free,
In dreams woven kindly, we're meant to be.

Guardians of wishes, these ancients stand tall,
Holding our fears, and our joys, one and all.
In their tranquil embrace, we learn to believe,
That dreams woven here are ours to achieve.

Ethereal Glow of Dusk's Ballet

As the sun dips low, a soft ballet starts,
Shadows embrace with their delicate arts.
The sky blazes amber, then deepens to gray,
In the ethereal glow, we linger and sway.

The horizon whispers a promise of night,
Drifting on twilight, a soft, gentle flight.
Stars emerge slowly, like dancers on stage,
Casting their light on the world, turning pages.

With each sighing breeze, stories take flight,
A canvas of dreams in the fading light.
The earth melts away into soft, muted hues,
In dusk's gentle ballet, we find our own cues.

Colors entwine like a lover's embrace,
Transforming the landscape, a wondrous grace.
As day breathes its last in a crystalline way,
We dance in the moments that dusk will convey.

In this ethereal glow, we learn to let go,
Finding our rhythm, surrendering slow.
As nightfall descends with its sweet, tender sway,
We revel in beauty, in dusk's lovely ballet.

Radiance in the Green Reverie

In the forest's gentle sway,
Leaves dance softly to the day,
Sunlight filters, golden beams,
Whispering of our wild dreams.

Amidst the blooms that brightly show,
Colors burst, a vibrant glow,
Nature sings, a sweet refrain,
Binding hearts in joy's domain.

Rustling branches, soft and near,
Awakening the soul's sincere,
With each breeze, a new delight,
Radiance captured in pure sight.

Carpets green beneath our feet,
Nature's pulse, a steady beat,
In this realm where shadows play,
Life's reflections find their way.

So linger here, in peace reside,
Where every moment feels like tide,
In the green, let spirits soar,
Radiance thriving evermore.

Whispers of Dewlit Enchantment

Morning breaks with gentle grace,
Dewdrops cling in nature's face,
Whispers float on tender air,
Magic lingers everywhere.

Petals quiver, soft and bright,
Glistening in the dawn's first light,
Singing songs of sweet embrace,
Time stands still in this warm space.

Fragrant breezes kiss our skin,
Whispers woven, soft within,
Every breath a love's caress,
Nature's touch, a boundless finesse.

As shadows dance on emerald ground,
Ancient stories all around,
In this moment, pure and true,
We find enchantment, me and you.

So let us wander, hearts aligned,
In the dew, our dreams defined,
Where time unfolds like petals rare,
Whispers of love fill the air.

Glimmers in the Twilight Canopy

As daylight fades to twilight's grace,
Stars begin their dance in space,
Beneath the tree's embracing arms,
A world awakens, filled with charms.

Shadows stretch and blush in hue,
Painting night with colors new,
Fireflies twinkle, soft and near,
Glimmers whisper, drawing near.

In the hush, a sigh of breeze,
Nature's breath, a gentle tease,
As night descends, the magic grows,
Filled with secrets only the heart knows.

The moon's soft glow, a silver thread,
Weaving tales of dreams long spread,
In the canopy's embrace, we glide,
Finding peace where hopes abide.

So hold this moment, close and dear,
Where glimmers spark and joy is clear,
In twilight's arms, let worries cease,
Glimmers in the night, our peace.

Secrets Beneath Starlit Bow

Underneath a starlit bow,
Whispers drift, soft and slow,
Night unfurls its velvet cloak,
As secrets shared become bespoke.

Gentle breezes, tales untold,
Embrace our hearts, as night unfolds,
Stars, like jewels, in endless sky,
Guard the dreams that float nearby.

Moonlight spills on silken ground,
Casting magic all around,
In this realm, where shadows sigh,
We chase the dusk, as moments fly.

With every heartbeat, we explore,
Whispers urging us for more,
Beneath the canopy of light,
We find our way through endless night.

So linger here, where wonders blend,
In secret worlds, our spirits mend,
Beneath the stars, our hearts shall vow,
To keep the secrets, beneath the bow.

Echoes of the Night's Symphony

Whispers of the night, softly play,
Stars in concert, in grand array.
Moonlight dances on silken waves,
As the world in slumber, gently saves.

Crickets chirp, a nightingale sings,
Melodies drift on delicate wings.
Each note a secret, tender and bright,
That threads through the fabric of the night.

Breezes carry the tales from afar,
Guiding the dreams where wishes are.
In this harmony, we find our peace,
In the night's embrace, all troubles cease.

Echoes of laughter, memories past,
In the darkness, shadows are cast.
Yet in this silence, hope shall ignite,
With whispers of love, in the night's light.

Beneath the stars, we close our eyes,
Cradled by moonbeams from the skies.
As the night breathes, together we flow,
In the symphony's embrace, we grow.

Cascade of Glimmers Above

Glistening jewels in the night sky,
Winking softly as they drift by.
Each star tells a story, a gleam,
Painting the heavens, a radiant dream.

Comets trail with a fiery grace,
Dancing through the vastness of space.
Galaxies swirl in a cosmic dance,
Inviting us all to dream and chance.

Nebulas bloom in colors so bold,
Whispering secrets of ages untold.
With every twinkle, hope is reborn,
In the warm embrace of the morning's dawn.

Beneath their light, we find our way,
Guided by dreams that never sway.
Their cascade of glimmers, a beacon bright,
Illuminating the path to our delight.

So look up high, let your spirit soar,
In the cascade of stars, forever explore.
The universe whispers, invites you near,
In the tapestry of light, feel no fear.

Mysteries of the Shadow Realm

Veils of mist in the twilight hour,
Encircle the trees, a mystical power.
Shadows linger, secrets they keep,
Whispering tales where the lost souls weep.

Figures dance in the flickering light,
Crafting illusions that flicker and fright.
Echoes of laughter, shivers of dread,
In the heart of the darkness, where dreams are dead.

Yet within the shadows, hope does bloom,
Though cloaked in silence, banishing gloom.
For every shadow holds a story untold,
A glimpse of the brave and the bold.

Step softly through the realm of the night,
For hidden wonders lie just within sight.
Unlock the secrets of what you find,
And embrace the mysteries that intertwine.

In the shadow's embrace, we learn and we grow,
With each moment cherished, wisdom will flow.
So journey onward, seek out the dream,
In the mystery's breath, let your heart beam.

Secrets Carried by the Wind

Whispers weaving through the tall trees,
Telling tales carried on the breeze.
Every rustle, a message of yore,
Each sigh of the wind opens a door.

Clouds drift lazily, sharing their dreams,
Painting the sky with shimmering beams.
In the soft gusts, secrets unfold,
Stories of lovers and treasures of gold.

The wind knows of journeys, both far and near,
Collecting the laughter, the joy, the fear.
In its embrace, we find our way,
Guided by whispers that drift and sway.

Dance with the breeze, let your spirit fly,
Feel the connection, let go of the sigh.
For in every gust, there's a world to explore,
A silent companion, forevermore.

Listen closely, the secrets it sings,
Of forgotten moments and wondrous things.
In the heart of the wind, we find our home,
With each gentle breath, we're never alone.

9 781805 597070